the To&Through project

District Overview

UCHICAGO**CCSR**
THE UNIVERSITY OF CHICAGO CONSORTIUM ON CHICAGO SCHOOL RESEARCH

I0163153

RESEARCH BRIEF DECEMBER 2014

The Educational Attainment of Chicago Public Schools Students

A Focus on Four-Year College Degrees

Kaleen Healey, Jenny Nagaoka, and Valerie Michelman

the To&Through project

The aim of The To&Through Project is to drive higher high school and college graduation rates. To reach that goal, families, policymakers, and educators need clear, actionable data on the milestones that research demonstrates are pivotal to success.

The To&Through Project is a three-part series of Urban Education Institute data reports and tools. It fills information gaps by highlighting critical points students encounter during their K-12 years that are strongly related to their likelihood of success in high school and college. The project sheds light on surprising findings and prompts additional questions. Focusing on the goal of college completion, To&Through equips stakeholders with a new depth of information, both across the district and for individual Chicago public schools. Reports are organized in a way that allow students, families, counselors, principals, admissions officers, higher education leaders, and others to make and support smarter decisions.

ACKNOWLEDGEMENTS

The authors gratefully acknowledge the many people who contributed to this brief. The content of this brief was shaped by valuable feedback provided by the Donors Forum College and Career Access, Persistence and Success Group and the UChicago CCSR College Success Report advisory board. CCSR Steering Committee members Brian Spittle and Raquel Farmer-Hinton offered very thoughtful reviews as we finalized the narrative. We are grateful for the technical support and data expertise provided by Thomas Kelley-Kemple and Will Hobart at CPS. We thank the members of CCSR's research review group, especially Elaine Allensworth, Penny Sebring, and Marisa de la Torre, and technical readers Matthew Holsapple and Julia Gwynne, for their helpful reviews. CCSR's communications team, including Emily Krone, Bronwyn McDaniel, and Jessica Puller, were instrumental in the production of this brief. We also thank Melissa Roderick and CCSR's postsecondary research team for providing the research base that guides this brief.

This work was supported by the Crown Family Philanthropies, the Bill and Melinda Gates Foundation, and an anonymous funder. We thank them for their support and collaboration with this project. We are also grateful for the operating grants from the Spencer Foundation and the Lewis-Sebring Family Foundation that support the work of UChicago CCSR.

This report was produced by UChicago CCSR's publications and communications staff: Emily Krone, Director for Outreach and Communication; Bronwyn McDaniel, Senior Manager for Outreach and Communication; and Jessica Puller, Communications Specialist.

Graphic Design: Jeff Hall Design
Photography: Lloyd DeGrane, Cynthia Howe, and David Schalliol
Editing: Ann Lindner

12.2014/350/jh.design@rcn.com

What Proportion of CPS Ninth-Graders Earn a Four-Year Degree?

Introduction

A four-year college degree increases a student's employment prospects and earning potential.[1] Given this importance, it is not surprising that 75 percent of Chicago Public Schools (CPS) high school students aspire to obtain at least a four-year college degree.[2] Yet, prior research showed that few achieved this goal: a 2006 University of Chicago Consortium on Chicago School Research (UChicago CCSR) report estimated that—based on high school graduation rates, college enrollment rates, and college graduation rates—just 8 percent of CPS ninth-graders would earn a bachelor's degree by the time they reached their mid-twenties.[3] This number was shockingly low to many people and served as a rallying cry to drastically improve the college success of Chicago's students. It also provided a baseline for examining changes in the educational attainment of CPS students over time.

This brief updates that statistic, which we call the *"degree attainment index"* and describes the changes in the key milestones that comprise it—high school graduation, four-year college enrollment, and bachelor's degree completion—that have occurred since the 2006 report. It also shows how CPS graduates' qualifications for college—high school GPAs and ACT scores—and the colleges they attend have changed during this time period.

The 2014 Degree Attainment Index

In 2006, UChicago CCSR's landmark report, *From High School to the Future: A First Look at Chicago Public School Graduates' College Enrollment, College Preparation, and Graduation from Four-Year Colleges*, estimated that of 100 CPS ninth-graders, just eight would earn a bachelor's degree by the time they reached their mid-twenties. We now refer to this estimate as a degree attainment index. It is not the rate at which any single cohort of CPS ninth-graders obtains a college degree; rather, it combines the most recent high school graduation, college enrollment, and college graduation rates into a single metric that can be tracked over time (see box, *Overview of Data and Methods Used in CCSR's 2014 Degree Attainment Index* on p.4).

The 2014 UChicago CCSR degree attainment index is 14 percent—that is, of 100 CPS ninth-graders, we estimate that 14 will earn a four-year college degree within 10 years of beginning high school. **Figure 1** illustrates how the high school graduation, college enrollment, and college graduation rates are combined to produce the 2014 degree attainment index. It begins with the CCSR high school graduation rate of 73 percent—that is, of 100 first-time ninth-graders, 73 will graduate from a CPS high school within four years. Among high school graduates, the four-year college enrollment rate is 40 percent. Therefore, of

---

1   Oreopoulos & Petronijevic (2013).
2   UChicago CCSR analysis of 2013 My Voice, My School student survey. We use the term *"four-year college"* to refer to institutions that primarily grant baccalaureate or post-baccalaureate degrees. We use the terms *"four-year college degree"* and *"bachelor's degree"* interchangeably in this brief to refer to degrees awarded by these institutions, even though we allow students six years to complete the degree. A future UChicago CCSR brief will examine trends in two-year college enrollment and degree attainment.
3   Roderick, Nagaoka, Allensworth, Coca, Correa, & Stoker (2006); Allensworth (2006). The degree attainment index in the 2006 report multiplied UChicago CCSR's most recently published five-year high school graduation rate (53 percent; first-time ninth-graders in 1994-95) by the four-year college

enrollment rate among high school graduates (32 percent; CPS graduating classes of 2002-04) by the six-year college graduation rate among four-year college enrollees (35 percent later updated to 45 percent; CPS graduating classes of 1998-99). The initial report (Roderick et al., 2006) estimated that 6 percent of ninth-graders would earn a four-year degree. This number was updated to 8 percent in Allensworth (2006), after the University of Illinois at Urbana-Champaign provided complete graduation records to the National Student Clearinghouse (NSC), the source used by UChicago CCSR for college enrollment and graduation data, and students attending Southern Illinois University Carbondale (SIUC) were removed from the analysis after SIUC officials indicated that they had provided only partial graduation records to the NSC.

FIGURE 1

CPS Students' Path to Attaining a Bachelor's Degree Within 10 Years of Beginning High School

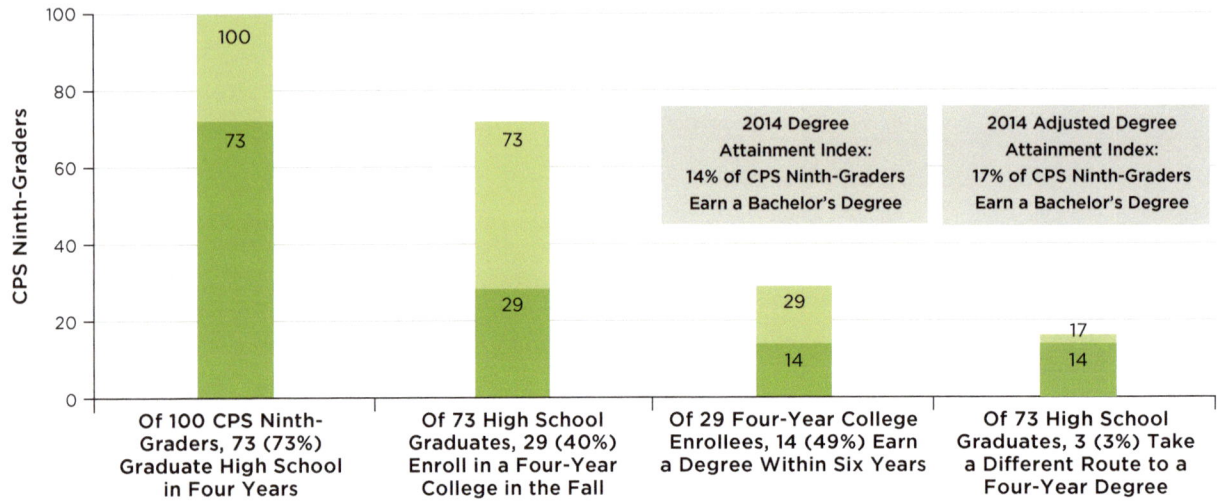

Note: Data and methods are described in Appendix B and in the box *Overview of Data and Methods Used in CCSR's 2014 Degree Attainment Index.*

the 73 ninth-graders who graduate high school, 40 percent (or 29 students) enroll in a four-year college in the fall after high school graduation. The six-year bachelor's degree completion rate for students who enroll in a four-year college is 49 percent. Of the 29 ninth-graders who graduated high school in four years and enrolled in a four-year college in the fall after high school graduation, 49 percent (or 14 students) earn a bachelor's degree within six years of high school graduation.

The degree attainment index provides a good estimate of the actual degree attainment rates of CPS students, but it captures only students who take a straightforward path to a bachelor's degree. Students must graduate high school in four years, make an immediate transition into a four-year college, and earn their bachelor's degree within six years to be included in one of the three rates that comprise the degree attainment

index. Examining the actual degree attainment rates of prior cohorts of first-time ninth-graders (those who began high school from 1999 to 2002) reveals that a small proportion of students take a different route to a four-year degree.[4] Specifically, 3 percent of high school graduates who do not immediately enroll in a four-year college (e.g., delay entry into college or enroll in a two-year college) go on to earn a bachelor's degree within six years of high school graduation. The *"adjusted degree attainment index"* accounts for these alternative routes and brings the percent of CPS ninth-graders who earn a four-year degree by the time they reach their mid-twenties up to 17. While we show the adjusted degree attainment index in **Figure 1**, the remainder of this brief focuses on the increase from 8 to 14 percent, as the increase to 17 percent is due to the adjustment that was not made in the 2006 report.

---

4 Enough time has passed that we can calculate the actual degree attainment rates for the students who began ninth grade from 1998-2002, which are among the cohorts studied in the 2006 report. Among these cohorts, 10 to 12 percent of students earned a four-year degree within 10 years of beginning high school, indicating that the 8 percent degree attainment index was an underestimate. The degree attainment index includes only the rate at which high school graduates enroll in four-year colleges in the fall following graduation. The actual degree attainment rates show that 81 percent of the students who earned a four-year degree within six years had enrolled in a four-year college in the fall following high school graduation, while 7 percent had enrolled in a two-year college and 12 percent had not enrolled in any college in the fall following high school graduation. Therefore, 14 percent is likely an underestimate of the degree attainment rate for current CPS students. If we assume that the four-year degree completion rates for CPS graduates who enroll in a four-year, two-year, and no college remain the same over time, the adjusted degree attainment index is 17 percent. If we retroactively apply this adjustment to the degree attainment index published in 2006, it changes from 8 to 9 percent.

The increase from 8 to 14 percent represents a substantial improvement and means that CPS is closing the gap with national degree attainment rates (see box, *How Does CPS's Degree Attainment Index of 14 Percent Compare to Other Places in the Country?*). Even with this improvement, however, there is still much work to be done to increase the rate at which CPS students graduate high school, enroll in college, and earn a bachelor's degree. As shown in **Figure 1**, one of the biggest stumbling blocks is the four-year college enrollment rate among students who graduate high school. Another concern is that only half of the students who do enroll in a four-year college manage to earn a degree within six years.

The remainder of this brief focuses on the changes in high school graduation, four-year college enrollment, and six-year college graduation that have occurred since the 2006 report. It then examines the changes in high school GPAs, ACT scores, and the colleges attended by CPS graduates that occurred during this time period.

How Does CPS's Degree Attainment Index of 14 Percent Compare to Other Places in the Country?

CPS's degree attainment index of 14 percent may seem extremely low, given that 75 percent of CPS high school students report that they want to obtain a four-year degree.[A] Yet, CPS does not appear to be far behind the degree attainment rates of students in other urban districts, or the nation as a whole.

Other urban districts report college degree attainment rates from 4 to 13 percent. Several districts have published the rates at which their ninth-graders earn college degrees. CPS's degree attainment index of 14 percent is similar to, or higher than, the rates in those districts. In Philadelphia, 10 percent of first-time ninth-graders in 1999 had earned a two- or four-year degree 10 years later.[B] The Washington, DC, public schools released a degree attainment index of 9 percent in 2006.[C] In 2010, Houston published a degree attainment index of 13 percent.[D] Recent studies from New York City and Baltimore provide high school graduation, four-year college enrollment and bachelor's degree completion rates that, when combined, produce degree attainment indexes of 11 and 4 percent, respectively.[E]

Nationally, less than a third of ninth-graders obtain a four-year college degree by their mid-twenties—the most comparable national estimate to the CPS index is 18 percent. The college completion rates for students in other urban school districts may seem low; but, as described below, the best estimate of a comparable national rate suggests that only about a fifth of students end up obtaining a bachelor's degree within 10 years of starting the ninth grade.

The most comparable number to the degree attainment index in **Figure 1** can be produced from national statistics on high school graduation, college enrollment, and college completion. These rates are not perfectly comparable because they use different calculations or represent different years than those used for **Figure 1**; however, they provide a general sense of the estimated degree attainment rates for students across the country. Nationally, the high school graduation rate is 81 percent,[F] the four-year college enrollment rate among high school graduates is 38 percent,[G] and the six-year college graduation rate among four-year college enrollees is 59 percent.[H] Multiplying these rates, as in **Figure 1** for CPS, produces an 18 percent national

A UChicago CCSR analysis of 2013 My Voice, My School student survey.
B Note that this is an actual degree attainment rate among ninth-graders in the School District of Philadelphia, not an index as reported for CPS in this brief; Snyder (2010, September 14).
C Haynes (2006, October 19).
D Mellon (2010, June 17); note that the index is for ninth-graders in the Houston Independent School District and it gives students only four and half years (instead of six, as in CCSR's index) to complete a four-year degree; Apollo Consulting Group, LLC (2010).
E Coca (2014); Durham & Olson (2013). Note that the bachelor's degree completion rate for New York City includes students who began at a four-year college and earned any degree (including a two-year degree), within four years (instead of six, as in CCSR's index).
F Stetser & Stillwell (2014). Unlike UChicago CCSR, NCES did not track students over time and instead estimated the *"averaged freshmen graduation rate,"* which divides the number of diplomas in a given year by the average of the number of eighth-graders five years prior, the number of ninth-graders four years prior, and the number of tenth-graders three years prior. This method is considered less accurate than the method used by CCSR.
G National Center for Education Statistics (2013e); this rate is likely an underestimate because it includes GED recipients in the denominator.
H National Center for Education Statistics (2013b).

degree attainment index. It suggests that the degree attainment index for CPS is probably lower than that of the nation, but it is not far below.

Other statistics that are available on national college completion rates overestimate the percent of ninth-graders who obtain a college degree by their mid-twenties; but these statistics provide confirmation that, nationally, less than a third of students earn a bachelor's degree within 10 years of beginning high school. One such statistic is the percent of adults in their mid/late-twenties who hold a bachelor's degree. In 2012, about a third (34 percent) of adults aged 25 to 29 nationwide held a bachelor's degree or higher.[I] The rates for African American and Latino adults were 23 and 15 percent, respectively. These rates are not comparable to CPS's degree attainment index because they give students several additional years to earn a degree, and include young adults who earned a GED instead of graduating from high school and young adults who did not complete their education in the United States. However, they suggest that, on average, high schools across the country are not close to getting even half of their ninth-graders to attain a four-year college degree.

The other estimate, also likely to be upwardly biased, comes from a longitudinal study that followed students for 10 years beginning when they were in tenth grade. Among a nationally representative sample of students who were in tenth grade in the spring of 2002, 33 percent earned a bachelor's degree by 2012.[J] The same study found that the bachelor's degree attainment rates for African American students and Latino students in the sample were 20 and 19 percent, respectively. However, the students for this study were selected at the end of tenth grade; the statistic does not account for students who had already dropped out or had not earned enough credits to be promoted to tenth grade. Furthermore, this study gives students two additional years to earn a degree than the statistics produced by UChicago CCSR. However, it also suggests that at the average high school in the United States, no more than a third of students obtain a college degree within 10 years of starting high school.

I   National Center for Education Statistics (2013d).

J   Lauff & Ingels (2014).

Overview of Data and Methods Used in CCSR's 2014 Degree Attainment Index

The percent of CPS ninth-graders who earn a four-year college degree is of interest to many people, but reporting actual degree attainment rates for a given cohort of ninth-graders provides an outdated assessment of CPS students' educational attainment. Using a four-year high school graduation rate and a six-year bachelor's degree rate, as we do here, gives students 10 years to progress through high school and college. Additional time is needed for students' college outcomes to be reported back to the district. The most recent group of students for whom we can track actual degree attainment rates were first-time ninth-graders in the 2002-03 school year. Thus an actual degree attainment rate is not very informative about current CPS students' educational prospects.

Instead, UChicago CCSR uses the following formula to create an index, or composite measure, of the most recently available rates for high school graduation, four-year college enrollment, and graduation from four-year colleges:

Degree Attainment Index = CCSR High School Graduation Rate x Four-Year College Enrollment Rate x Six-Year College Graduation Rate from Four-Year Colleges

Using this method means that our high school graduation rate will come from a cohort of students who recently graduated high school, while our college graduation rate will come from a cohort of students who graduated high school several years ago. This is the same method used in the 2006 report, but we now refer to this number as the *"degree attainment index"* to distinguish it from actual degree attainment rates. CCSR's degree attainment index is calculated by multiplying three rates, each of which is explained below. More detailed information about the data and methods is provided in **Appendix B**.

CCSR High School Graduation Rate

The proportion of first-time ninth-graders who graduate high school in four years. The 2014 degree attainment index uses the high school graduation rate for the students who were first-time ninth-graders in the 2010-11 school year and who graduated high school by fall 2014. CCSR's high school graduation rates differ from those published by CPS. The primary difference is that CCSR does not require verification for students who transfer out of the district. While CPS treats unverified transfers as dropouts in their publicly reported graduation rates, CCSR treats all transfers as true transfers and not dropouts. This decision was made because CPS's verification system is very strict, and CCSR analysis of the students coded as unverified transfers suggested they were more similar to verified transfer students than to dropouts.[K] Some students listed as transfers may have dropped out and some unverified transfers may be enrolled in another school. This means that CCSR's high school graduation rate is likely an overestimate, while CPS's rate is likely an underestimate.

Four-Year College Enrollment Rate

The proportion of high school graduates who enroll in a four-year college in the fall following high school graduation. The four-year college enrollment rate used in the 2014 degree attainment index is of students who graduated from CPS in the 2012-13 school year (including summer graduates). Those who enrolled in a four-year college in fall 2013 are considered four-year college enrollees. Graduates of alternative and special education schools are not

included in these rates. Data on college enrollment come from the National Student Clearinghouse (NSC), which houses enrollment and graduation records for colleges throughout the United States and covers 98 percent of all postsecondary enrollments nationally.[L]

Six-Year College Graduation Rate

The proportion of four-year college enrollees who earn a bachelor's degree within six years. The college graduation rate for the 2014 degree attainment index is of four-year college enrollees from the CPS graduating class of 2006. Students who earned a bachelor's degree by mid-September 2012 are counted as college graduates. Data on college graduation come from the NSC. Students who enroll in a college which does not provide graduation records to the NSC in the fourth through sixth years after high school graduation are not included in these rates as we are unable to determine if they earned a degree.[M] Since the 2006 report, NSC has changed how they match CPS graduates to college records. The new algorithm matches slightly more CPS graduates to college enrollment and graduation records, which has a slight effect on the increases in the college graduation rates reported in this brief. The high school graduating classes of 2003 and later are affected by the new algorithm.

CCSR Adjusted Degree Attainment Index

The *"adjusted degree attainment index"* takes into account the proportion of CPS graduates who earned a four-year degree but did not enroll in a four-year college in the fall after high school graduation. For the graduating classes of 2003-06, 7 percent of students who enrolled in a two-year college and 4 percent of students who did not enroll in any college in the fall following high school graduation went on to earn a bachelor's degree within six years of high school graduation. Multiplying these rates by the proportion of 2013 CPS graduates who enroll in two-year colleges (21 percent) and no college (39 percent), respectively, produces the 3 percentage point adjustment.

K   Allensworth (2005).
L   National Student Clearinghouse (n.d.).
M   The number of four-year college enrollees removed from

the college graduation rate calculation is 554 (14 percent) for the CPS graduating class of 2000 and 93 (2 percent) for the CPS graduating class of 2006.

What Accounts for the Increase from 8 to 14 Percent?

The increase in the degree attainment index from 8 to 14 percent has been driven largely by the increasing rates at which CPS students are graduating high school and enrolling in four-year colleges. The college graduation rate among students who enroll in a four-year college has increased only slightly, but there are many more students graduating high school and enrolling in college. These increases mean that among the roughly 28,000 first-time ninth-graders, nearly 1,700 more students are estimated to earn a degree. This section details the changes that occurred in high school graduation, college enrollment, and college graduation from 2006 to 2014.[5]

The CCSR four-year high school graduation rate has increased substantially (see Figure 2). The CCSR high school graduation rate has increased by 15 percentage points—from 58 percent in 2006 to 73 percent in 2014.[6]

- Graduation rates have improved for students at all levels of incoming high school achievement—in fact, the biggest increases have been among students with the lowest ninth-grade standardized test scores (see Appendix A). High school graduation rates have also improved for students of all races/ethnicities and for both genders (see Table 1).

- The CPS graduation rate has improved more than the most comparable national rate, which increased from 73 percent in 2006 to 81 percent in 2012.[7]

- The upward trend in high school graduation is likely to continue; 84 percent of ninth-graders in 2013-14 were on-track to graduate, compared to 73 percent in 2010-11 (who should have graduated in 2014).[8]

FIGURE 2

CCSR Four-Year High School Graduation Rates Among First-Time Ninth-Graders

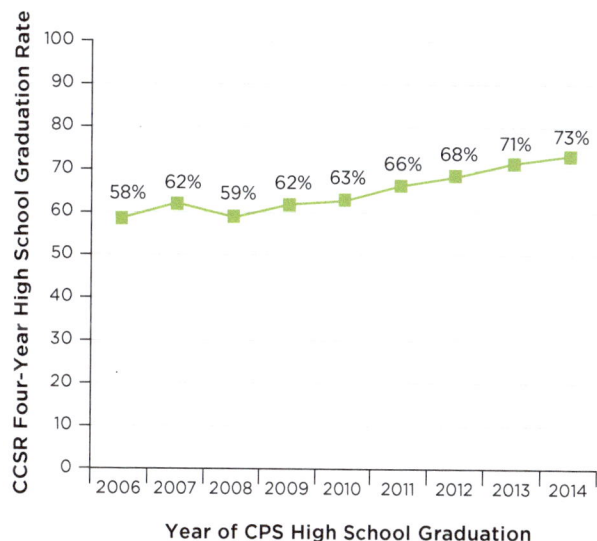

Note: Data and methods are described in Appendix B.

The four-year college enrollment rate has increased moderately (see Figure 3). The four-year college enrollment rate for CPS graduates has increased by 7 percentage points, from 33 percent in 2006 to 40 percent in 2013.[9]

---

5 The 2006 rates displayed in this section are not the rates published in the 2006 study, but rather the rates from the time the study was published. See Footnote 3 for more information about the rates in the 2006 report.

6 CCSR's high school graduation rate differs from that published by the district, primarily due to how students who transfer out of the district are handled (see box, *Overview of Data and Methods Used in CCSR's 2014 Degree Attainment Index* and Appendix B for more information). CPS's published four-year high school graduation rate increased from 50 percent in 2006 to 62 percent in 2013; a 2014 four-year rate has not been published by the district (Chicago Public Schools, n.d.).

7 National Center for Education Statistics (2013a); Stetser & Stillwell (2014). While the NCES rates are the best available national comparison, the comparison should be interpreted cautiously as the rates are not truly comparable due to how they are calculated. See Footnote F on p.3 for more information on the limitations of the rate.

8 Chicago Public Schools (n.d.); Roderick, Kelley-Kemple, Johnson, & Beechum (2014). On-track ninth-graders are nearly four times as likely to graduate as those who are off-track.

9 The two-year college enrollment rate for CPS graduates also increased from 16 percent in 2006 to 21 percent in 2013.

FIGURE 3

Enrollment Rates at Four-Year Colleges Among High School Graduates

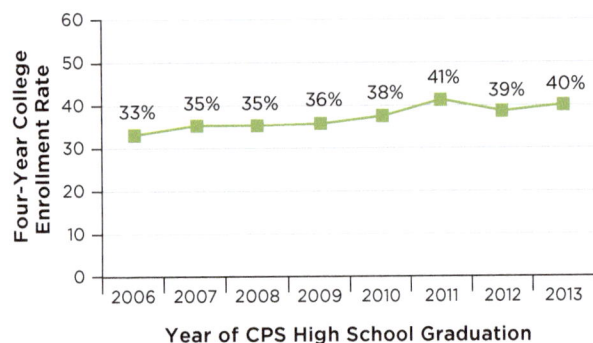

Year of CPS High School Graduation

Note: Data and methods are described in Appendix B.

- Four-year college enrollment rates have increased for all races/ethnicities (**see Table 1**), for both genders (**see Table 1**), and for CPS graduates with a GPA of 2.5 or higher (**see Appendix A**).

  - Still, over a quarter of students with a high school GPA of 3.5 or better and over a third of students with a 3.0-3.4 GPA do not enroll in a four-year college in the fall after high school graduation.

  - One fifth of students who scored a 24 or better on the ACT and over a third who scored 21-23 still do not enroll in a four-year college in the fall after high school graduation.

- The four-year college enrollment rate for CPS graduates has increased more than the most comparable national rate. Nationally, enrollment in four-year colleges decreased from 41 percent in 2006 to 38 percent in 2012.[10]

In recent years, the college graduation rate among four-year college enrollees has increased only slightly (**see Figure 4**). The six-year college graduation rate for four-year college enrollees increased by 6 percentage points between the CPS graduating classes of 2000 and 2004 and by 2 percentage points between the CPS graduating classes of 2003 and 2006.[11]

- We present two separate lines for college graduation rates due to a change in how CPS graduates were matched to college enrollment and graduation records by the NSC.[12] We can produce graduation rates from both versions of the matching algorithm for the CPS graduating classes of 2003 and 2004.

- Because both lines show slight increases and we have overlapping data for two years, we estimate that there has been little change in college graduation rates—especially in recent years.

- Nationally, there have been small changes in six-year bachelor's degree completion rates from 2000 to 2006: from 58 to 59 percent for four-year college enrollees.[13]

FIGURE 4

Six Year Bachelor's Degree Completion Rates Among Four-Year College Enrollees

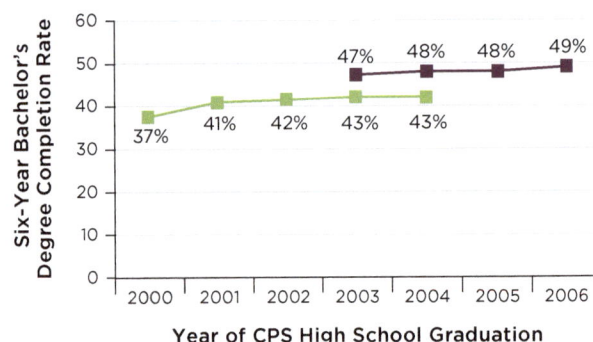

Year of CPS High School Graduation

Note: Data and methods are described in Appendix B. The green line represents the degree completion rate using an older version of NSC's matching algorithm and the purple line represents the degree completion rate using an updated version of the algorithm.

---

10 Nationally, enrollment in two-year colleges increased from 25 percent in 2006 to 29 percent in 2012. National college enrollment rates are not available for 2013. The rates shown are from National Center for Education Statistics (2013e) and, unlike UChicago CCSR's rates, include GED recipients in the denominator.

11 Among two-year college enrollees, 9 percent earned a certificate or degree within three years in 2006 (2003 CPS graduates), compared to 8 percent in 2012 (2009 CPS graduates). Limitations of the NSC data prevent us from distinguishing students who earned an associate's degree from students who completed a certificate or less than

two-year degree program at a two-year college. Nationally, the graduation rate for two-year college enrollees increased from 29 percent in 2006 to 31 percent in 2012 (National Center for Education Statistics, 2013c).

12 In 2012, the records for the CPS graduating classes of 2003 through 2011 were *"rematched"* by the NSC using an updated version of their matching algorithm. The rematching did not systematically impact enrollment records. However, the rematched records, and all following records, contain more records of degrees.

13 National Center for Education Statistics (2013b).

8

TABLE 1

Changes in Educational Attainment Rates by Race/Ethnicity and Gender, 2006 to 2014

	CCSR Four-Year High School Graduation Rate Among First-Time Ninth-Graders		Four-Year College Enrollment Rate Among High School Graduates		Six-Year College Graduation Rate Among Four-Year College Enrollees		Degree Attainment Index	
	2006	2014	2006	2013	2009	2012	2006	2014
Latino Males (22% of 2013-14 first-time ninth-graders)	52%	**74%**	21%	**30%**	40%	**51%**	4%	**11%**
Latino Females (22% of 2013-14 first-time ninth-graders)	67%	**83%**	26%	**37%**	46%	**51%**	8%	**16%**
African American Males (21% of 2013-14 first-time ninth-graders)	42%	**57%**	29%	**34%**	33%	**32%**	4%	**6%**
African American Females (21% of 2013-14 first-time ninth-graders)	61%	**71%**	36%	**44%**	41%	**41%**	9%	**13%**
White Males (4% of 2013-14 first-time ninth-graders)	65%	**81%**	42%	**52%**	61%	**64%**	17%	**27%**
White Females (4% of 2013-14 first-time ninth-graders)	76%	**88%**	48%	**59%**	61%	**70%**	22%	**36%**
Asian Males (2% of 2013-14 first-time ninth-graders)	80%	**89%**	56%	**60%**	62%	**66%**	28%	**35%**
Asian Females (2% of 2013-14 first-time ninth-graders)	89%	**95%**	60%	**67%**	67%	**69%**	36%	**44%**

Note: 2013 college enrollment rates and 2012 college graduation rates are the most recent available. We show the 2009 college graduation rates, rather than 2006, because the underlying data were matched by the NSC using the same algorithm as the data used for the 2012 college graduation rate. This slightly understates changes since 2006 in the college graduation rates and the degree attainment indexes. The degree attainment indexes by race and gender do not include the adjustment for students who take a less straightforward route to a four-year degree, so the indexes shown here are likely underestimates of actual attainment rates.

9

Educational Attainment by Race/Ethnicity and Gender

While the increases in the rates that comprise the degree attainment index are marks of progress, there remains considerable variation in these by students' race/ethnicity and gender. This section shows how changes in high school graduation, four-year college enrollment, and six-year college graduation vary by race/ethnicity and gender. This variation can be used to target supports for groups of students based on where they are likely to fall off the path from ninth grade to a bachelor's degree.

As shown in **Table 1,** high school graduation and four-year college enrollment rates improved for both males and females and for all racial/ethnic groups. However, in both 2006 and 2014, white and Asian students had higher high school graduation rates than African American and Latino students, and females had higher high school graduation rates than males. Similarly, in both 2006 and

2013, white and Asian CPS graduates had higher four-year college enrollment rates than African American and Latino graduates, and female graduates had higher enrollment rates than male graduates. The gender gap in high school graduation rates has become smaller over time, while the gender gap in four-year college enrollment has grown larger over time. With the exception of African American students, college graduation rates have improved for students of all races/ethnicities and for both genders. white and Asian students continue to have higher college graduation rates than African American and Latino students.

The disparities in high school graduation, college enrollment, and college graduation produce large differences in the degree attainment index. In particular, the degree attainment index for African American males is 6 percent. Asian females have the highest degree attainment index at 44 percent. For all groups, the degree attainment index is less than 50 percent.

Table 1 also shows how different rates for high school graduation, college enrollment, and college graduation can produce similar degree attainment indexes. For example, Latino males and African American females have similar degree attainment indexes, but for different reasons. Latino males enroll in four-year colleges at a lower rate than African American females; but among those students who enroll, Latino males graduate from college at a higher rate.

10

Have Students' Qualifications and the Colleges They Attend Changed?

Have Students' Qualifications and Preparation for College Improved?

Prior UChicago CCSR research shows that cumulative high school GPA and ACT score are the student qualifications that are most predictive of college success.[14] High ACT scores are an important qualification for college admission, and they give students access to more selective colleges. This is important because institutional graduation rates tend to be higher at more selective colleges. High school GPA is a strong indicator of students' preparation for college; only four-year college enrollees with a high school GPA of 3.0 or higher have at least a 50 percent probability of earning a degree within six years.[15] Even among students with the same ACT scores, there is wide variation in their likelihood of earning a bachelor's degree by their high school GPA (see Appendix C).

CPS graduates' college qualifications have not declined even though many more students are graduating, meaning the increase in high school graduation rates has not come at the expense of students' preparation for college. In fact, the average ACT score and GPA for CPS graduates have gone up, while many more

students are graduating.[16] Still, the average graduate does not have the qualifications needed to be likely to succeed in college. This section shows how ACT scores and high school GPAs have changed since 2006.

The average ACT score for CPS graduates has improved (see Figure 5).

- As Figure 5 shows, for the class of 2013, the average ACT composite score was 18.4, compared to 17.6 for the class of 2006.[17] This increase occurred while nearly 5,500 additional students were taking the ACT: 64 percent of the 2002 first-time ninth-graders (who should have graduated in 2006) took the ACT, while 82 percent of the 2009 first-time ninth-graders (who should have graduated in 2013) did so.

- The proportion of graduates scoring 21 or better increased from 23 percent in 2006 to 30 percent in 2013.[18]

- At the same time, there has been a decrease in the proportion of graduates scoring below 18, from 56 percent in 2006 to 49 percent in 2013. When coupled with low GPAs, these students have limited college options.[19]

---

14 Roderick et al. (2006); Roderick, Nagaoka, Cocoa, Moeller, Roddie, Gilliam, & Patton (2008).

15 Roderick et al. (2006); Roderick, Holsapple, Kelley-Kemple, Johnson, & Moeller (forthcoming); Bowen, Chingos, & McPherson (2009).

16 The fact that achievement has not decreased substantially with so many more students making it to graduation also highlights two common misperceptions—that only low-achieving students drop out of CPS and that increasing graduation rates are driven by teachers passing students who otherwise would have failed.

17 The ACT score statistics shown here reflect the scores that CPS students received when they took the ACT as part of the

Prairie State Achievement Examination. These statistics are likely underestimates of CPS students' performance submitted in college applications because they do not reflect the higher scores that students who retake the exam may have submitted to colleges. These statistics differ from those published by CPS because they reflect the scores of graduates and not of all students who take the ACT.

18 The proportion of graduates without an ACT score also decreased substantially, so the increase is not accounted for by academically weaker students not taking the test.

19 Students who graduate high school with a GPA of less than 2.0 and an ACT score below 18 are likely to have access only to two-year colleges; Roderick et al. (2008).

FIGURE 5

ACT Composite Scores Among CPS High School Graduates

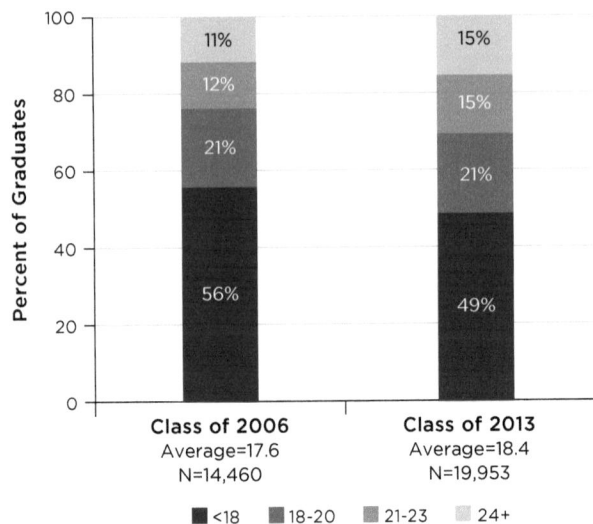

Class of 2006
Average=17.6
N=14,460

Class of 2013
Average=18.4
N=19,953

■ <18   ■ 18-20   ■ 21-23   ■ 24+

Note: Percentages and Ns do not include students with missing information (1,791 in 2006 and 593 in 2013).

FIGURE 6

Unweighted Cumulative GPA in Core Courses Among CPS High School Graduates

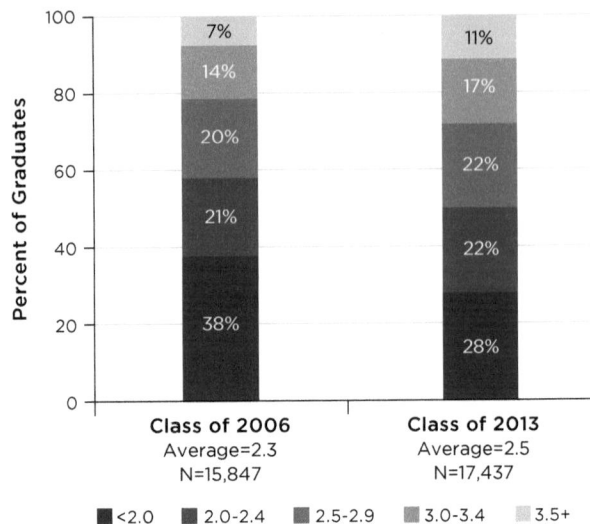

Class of 2006
Average=2.3
N=15,847

Class of 2013
Average=2.5
N=17,437

■ <2.0   ■ 2.0-2.4   ■ 2.5-2.9   ■ 3.0-3.4   ■ 3.5+

Note: Percentages and Ns do not include charter school graduates or students with missing data (404 in 2006 and 3,109 in 2013). Course grades for charter school students are not available.

The average cumulative GPA has improved slightly among students who were not enrolled in charter schools (see Figure 6).

- As Figure 6 shows, the average unweighted cumulative GPA in core courses for the graduating class of 2013 was 2.5, compared to 2.3 for the class of 2006.[20]

- There has been an increase in the proportion of graduates earning a 3.0 GPA or better, from 21 percent in 2006 to 28 percent in 2013. The proportion of students graduating with less than a 2.0 GPA has decreased from 38 percent of 2006 graduates to 28 percent of 2013 graduates.

- Still, fewer than a third of 2013 graduates have GPAs (greater than a 3.0) that give them at least a 50 percent chance of graduating college in six years, and under a third of students graduate with a GPA (less than 2.0) that gives them a 10 percent chance or less of graduating from college, if they even enroll.[21]

- The changes in GPA should be interpreted with some caution, as course grades are not available for

students enrolled in charter schools. Charter school graduates represented 15 percent of the class of 2013, compared to 2 percent of the class of 2006; this could affect the trends in GPA if charter school students have higher or lower GPAs, on average.

Are Students Enrolling in Colleges Where They Are Likely to Graduate?

In addition to CPS students' qualifications and preparation for college, the colleges they attend make a large difference in predicting whether they earn a degree. In fact, college choice makes the biggest difference for the college graduation prospects of the most highly qualified CPS graduates.[22] UChicago CCSR research shows that students with the same qualifications upon leaving high school are much more likely to graduate if they attend a college with a high institutional graduation rate.[23] When students attend a college where less than a quarter of all students graduate, chances are they will not graduate either—even if they have strong qualifications. This section shows how the colleges where CPS

---

20 Only GPAs that are based on four or more semester credits at a non-charter high school are included.

21 Roderick et al. (2006).

22 Roderick et al. (2006); Allensworth (2006).

23 Roderick et al. (2006); Allensworth (2006); Roderick et al. (forthcoming).

graduates enroll have changed since 2006. Changes in college match rates for CPS graduates are shown in **Appendix A.**

2013 CPS four-year college enrollees were more likely to enroll in colleges with institutional graduation rates of 50 percent or higher (see Figure 7).

• The proportion of four-year enrollees attending colleges with six-year institutional graduation rates of 50 percent or better increased from 58 percent in 2006 to 63 percent in 2013.

• In 2013, 37 percent of four-year college enrollees attended colleges with institutional graduation rates under 50 percent, compared to 44 percent in 2006. In these colleges, less than half of all students who enroll—not just CPS graduates—complete a degree within six years.

The institutional graduation rates at the colleges that CPS students frequently attend have improved, but remain low.

• Institutional graduation rates vary among colleges, even within the same selectivity category.

• While most of the top 10 colleges frequently attended by CPS graduates have improved their institutional and underrepresented minority graduation rates over the past six years, they remain low at many schools; at four of the top 10 four-year colleges, the institutional graduation rate remains below 50 percent (see **Table 2**).[24] Among 2013 four-year college enrollees, 47 percent were enrolled in one of these 10 colleges.

• Seven of the top 10 colleges had underrepresented minority (URM) graduation rates below 50 percent in both 2006 and 2012.[25] The college graduation rates for CPS graduates tend to mirror the URM graduation rates at the colleges they attend. The last column of **Table 2** shows the graduation rates of CPS graduates from the classes of 2000-06 at the top 10 colleges attended by this group of students.

FIGURE 7

Six-Year Institutional Graduation Rates at Colleges Attended by 2006 and 2013 Four-Year College Enrollees

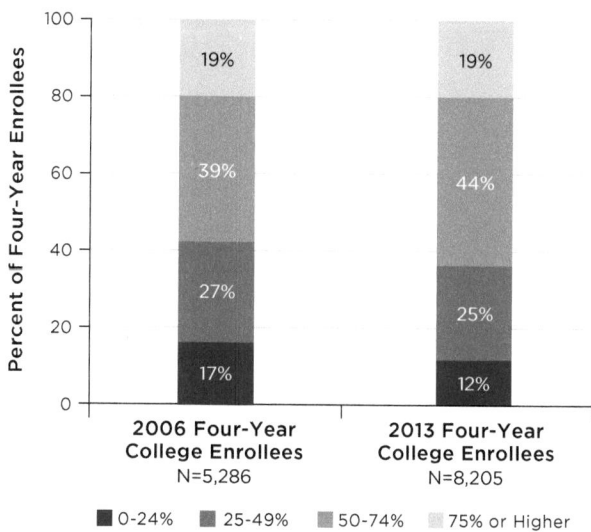

Note: Institutional graduation rates are from 2009. Percentages and Ns do not include students with missing information (45 in 2006 and 20 in 2013). Percentages do not add up to 100% due to rounding.

---

24 Robert Morris University and DeVry University are not included on this list because they offer both two- and four-year degree programs, and we are unable to distinguish whether students are enrolled in a two- or four-year program. On average, 186 CPS graduates enroll in Robert Morris each fall and 142 enroll at DeVry.

25 Underrepresented minority graduation rates include African American, Latino, and Native American students. Institutional and underrepresented minority graduation rates are publicly available and can be compared at http://www.collegeresults.org.

TABLE 2

Top 10 Four-Year Colleges Attended by 2006-13 CPS Graduates

College Name	Average Number of Fall Enrollees from CPS per Year 2006-13	Selectivity Category	2006 Six-Year Institutional Graduation Rate	2012 Six-Year Institutional Graduation Rate	2006 Six-Year URM Graduation Rate	2012 Six-Year URM Graduation Rate	Six-Year Graduation Rate for All CPS Four-Year Enrollees, 2006-12 (2000-06 CPS graduates)
University of Illinois at Chicago	708	Selective	51%	58%	39%	47%	49%
Northeastern Illinois University	541	Somewhat Selective	19%	21%	16%	17%	23%
University of Illinois at Urbana-Champaign	520	Very Selective	82%	84%	68%	72%	75%
Northern Illinois University	408	Somewhat Selective	48%	54%	38%	32%	30%
Southern Illinois University Carbondale*	341	Somewhat Selective	42%	48%	30%	31%	—
DePaul University	267	Selective	64%	68%	53%	61%	65%
Chicago State University	223	Somewhat Selective	18%	21%	19%	20%	18%
Columbia College Chicago	179	Nonselective	35%	41%	22%	30%	30%
Western Illinois University	155	Somewhat Selective	56%	54%	46%	45%	42%
Illinois State University	120	Selective	64%	71%	53%	50%	56%

Note: The average number of fall enrollees only includes college freshmen who graduated from CPS in the previous school year. Institutional and URM graduation rates are from College Results Online (2014). Selectivity categories are based on *Barron's* (2012). See Roderick et al. (2006) for details on how *Barron's* ratings compare to selectivity categories.

* After the 2006 report was published, Southern Illinois University Carbondale (SIUC) officials indicated that they did not provide complete graduation records to the NSC. The NSC website shows that SIUC began participating in NSC's Degree Verify program in 2008, and we are unable to confirm whether graduation records that appear in the NSC data before that time are complete. We therefore do not calculate a CPS graduation rate for SIUC.

Implications

From 2006 to 2014, CPS nearly doubled the proportion of ninth-graders who are estimated to earn a four-year college degree within 10 years of beginning high school. This is an important accomplishment and means that CPS is closing the gap with national degree attainment rates. The increase was driven largely by a substantial rise in the high school graduation rate and, to a lesser extent, by modest increases in the college enrollment and college graduation rates. This section highlights a number of areas for Chicago to work on to continue these improvements:

- Improving the high school graduation rate should remain a priority, especially for African American males whose graduation rate is still below 60 percent. Moreover—with the exception of Asian students—no racial/ethnic group has high school graduation rates above 90 percent, although all groups have shown improvements.

- Too few students graduate high school with at least a 3.0 GPA, which is what is needed to be likely to succeed in college. Almost a third of graduates leave school with a GPA of less than 2.0, which means they are not showing the skills needed for success in either college or the workforce. Students need to be supported in earning high grades while they are in high school. The skills and behaviors that earn students high grades—coming to class, completing their assignments, and meeting their teachers' expectations—are needed to succeed in college and in their careers.

- Many students with strong qualifications are not enrolling in college. Over a quarter of students with high school GPAs above 3.5 do not enroll in a four-year college in the fall after graduating high school.

- Students and their families need guidance in selecting a college where the student is likely to graduate. Many factors go into choosing a college, but the institutional graduation rate is one of the most important characteristics of colleges that students, families, and counselors should be paying attention to when making that choice.

- CPS students' college graduation rates are limited by the set of colleges from which they can choose to attend. Too many colleges have institutional and URM graduation rates below 50 percent, including many of the colleges frequently attended by CPS graduates. This suggests the need for postsecondary institutions to develop better mechanisms to support the students they admit in obtaining a degree.

15

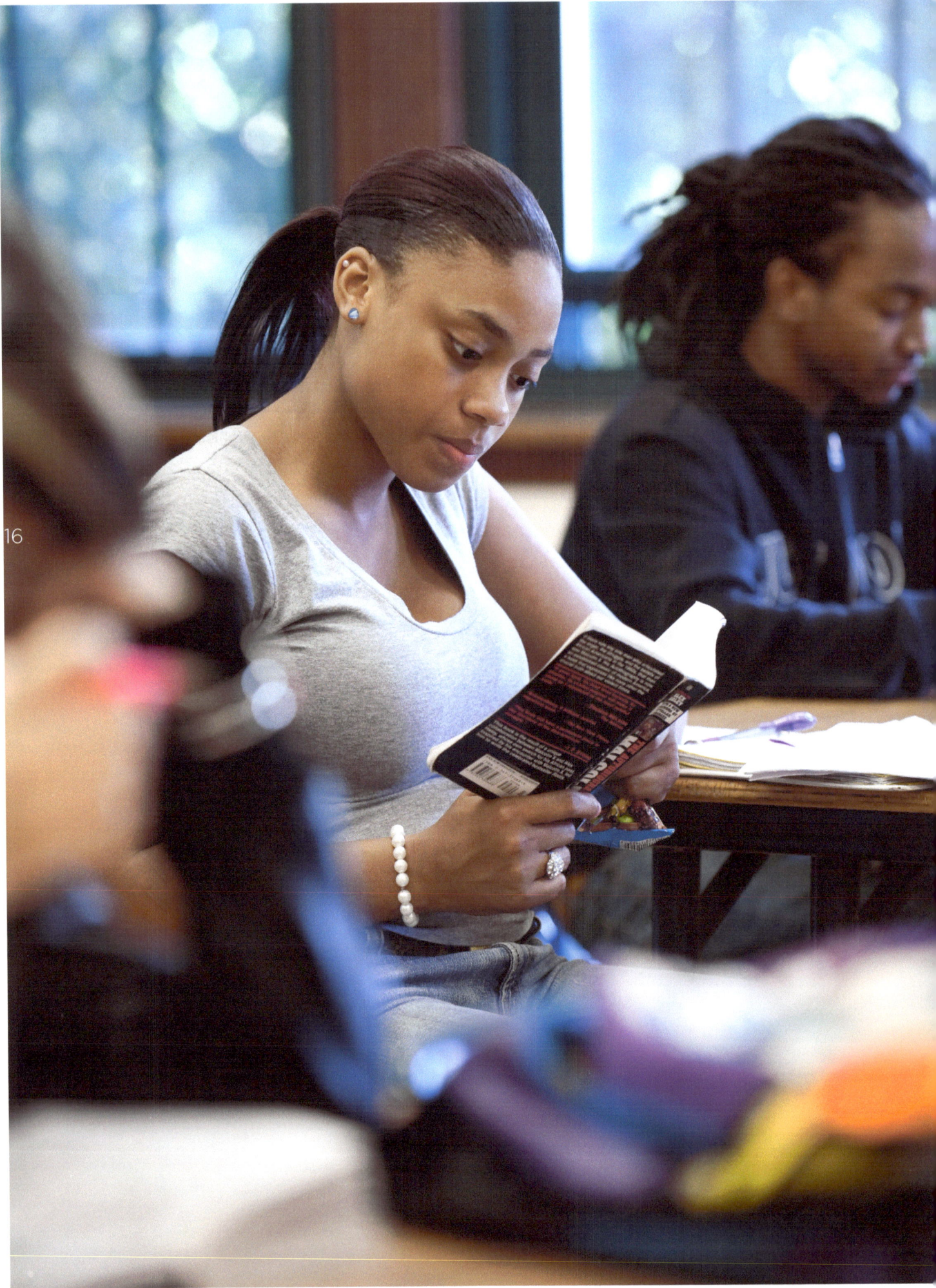

References

Allensworth, E. (2005).
Graduation and dropout trends in Chicago: A look at cohorts of students from 1991 through 2004. Chicago, IL: University of Chicago Consortium on Chicago School Research.

Allensworth, E. (2006).
Update to: From high school to the future: A first look at Chicago Public School graduates' college enrollment, college preparation, and graduation from four-year colleges. Chicago, IL: University of Chicago Consortium on Chicago School Research.

Apollo Consulting Group, LLC. (2010).
A community effort to transform HISD: Update to the Board of Education. [PowerPoint slides]. Retrieved from http://www.scribd.com/doc/33183044/HISD-strategic-plan-update

Barron's Educational Series, I.C.D. (2012).
Barron's profiles of American colleges 2013. Hauppauge, NY: Barron's Educational Series.

Bowen, W.G., Chingos, M.M., & McPherson, M.S. (2009).
Crossing the finish line: Completing college at America's public universities. Princeton, NJ: Princeton University Press.

Chicago Public Schools. (n.d.).
School data. Retrieved from http://cps.edu/SchoolData/Pages/SchoolData.aspx

Coca, V. (2014).
New York City goes to college: A first look at patterns of college enrollment, persistence and degree attainment for New York City high school students. New York, NY: Research Alliance for New York City Schools.

College Results Online. (2014).
Graduation Rates 2011 6-Year Grad Rate [data file]. Retrieved from http://www.collegeresults.org/

Durham, R.E., & Olson, L.S. (2013).
College enrollment and degree completion for Baltimore City graduates through the class of 2012. Baltimore, MD: Baltimore Education Research Consortium.

Haynes, V.D. (2006, October 18).
Bleak college graduation rate found. *The Washington Post.* Retrieved from http://www.washingtonpost.com/wp-dyn/content/article/2006/10/18/AR2006101801790.html

Lauff, E., & Ingels, S.J. (2014).
Education longitudinal study of 2002 (ELS:2002): A first look at 2002 high school sophomores 10 years later. (NCES # 2014363). U.S. Department of Education. Washington, DC: National Center for Education Statistics. Retrieved from http://nces.ed.gov/pubsearch/pubsinfo.asp?pubid=2014363

Mellon, E. (2010, June 17).
Only 15 percent of HISD freshmen graduate college—updated. *Houston Chronicle.* Retrieved from http://blog.chron.com/k12zone/2010/06/only-15-percent-of-hisd-freshmen-graduate-college-updated/

National Center for Education Statistics. (2013a).
Averaged freshman graduation rates for public secondary schools, by state or jurisdiction: Selected years, 1990-91 through 2009-10 [data file]. U.S. Department of Education. Washington, DC: National Center for Education Statistics. Retrieved from http://nces.ed.gov/programs/digest/d12/tables/dt12_124.asp

National Center for Education Statistics. (2013b).
Graduation rates of first-time bachelor's degree-seeking students at 4-year postsecondary institutions, by race/ethnicity, time to completion, sex, and control of institution: Selected cohort entry years, 1996 through 2006 [data file]. U.S. Department of Education. Washington, DC: National Center for Education Statistics. Retrieved from http://nces.ed.gov/programs/digest/d13/tables/dt13_326.10.asp

National Center for Education Statistics. (2013c).
Graduation rates of first-time degree/certificate-seeking students at 2-year postsecondary institutions who completed a credential within 150 percent of normal time, by race/ethnicity, sex, and control of institution: Selected cohort entry years, 2000 through 2009 [data file]. U.S. Department of Education. Washington, DC: National Center for Education Statistics. Retrieved from http://nces.ed.gov/programs/digest/d13/tables/dt13_326.20.asp

National Center for Education Statistics. (2013d).
Percentage of persons 25 to 29 years old with selected levels of educational attainment, by race/ethnicity and sex: Selected years, 1920 through 2012 [data file]. U.S. Department of Education. Washington, DC: National Center for Education Statistics. Retrieved from http://nces.ed.gov/programs/digest/d12/tables/dt12_009.asp

National Center for Education Statistics. (2013e). *Recent high school completers and their enrollment in 2-year and 4-year colleges, by sex: 1960 through 2012* [data file]. U.S. Department of Education. Washington, DC: National Center for Education Statistics. Retrieved from http://nces.ed.gov/programs/digest/d13/tables/dt13_302.10.asp

National Student Clearinghouse. (n.d.). *Who we are.* Retrieved from http://www.studentclearinghouse.org/about/

Oreopoulos, P., & Petronijevic, U. (2013). *Making college worth it: A review of research on the returns to higher education.* Washington, DC: National Bureau of Economic Research.

Roderick, M., Holsapple, M., Kelley-Kemple, T., Johnson, D.W., & Moeller, E. (forthcoming). *From high school to the future: College readiness and getting to graduation.* Chicago, IL: University of Chicago Consortium on Chicago School Research.

Roderick, M., Kelley-Kemple, T., Johnson, D.W., & Beechum, N.O. (2014). *Preventable failure: Improvements in long-term outcomes when high schools focused on ninth grade year: Research summary.* Chicago, IL: University of Chicago Consortium on Chicago School Research.

Roderick, M., Nagaoka, J., Allensworth, E., Coca, V., Correa, M., & Stoker, G. (2006). *From high school to the future: A first look at Chicago Public School graduates' college enrollment, college preparation, and graduation from four-year colleges.* Chicago, IL: University of Chicago Consortium on Chicago School Research.

Roderick, M., Nagaoka, J., Coca, V., Moeller, E., Roddie, K., Gillam, J., & Patton, D. (2008). *From high school to the future: Potholes on the road to college.* Chicago, IL: University of Chicago Consortium on Chicago School Research.

Snyder, S. (2010, September 14). New Phila. campaign aims to increase college graduation rate. *Philly.com.* Retrieved from http://articles.philly.com/2010-09-14/news/24974728_1_dropout-rate-first-time-ninth-graders-college-application-process

Stetser, M.C., & Stillwell, R. (2014). *Public high school four-year on-time graduation rates and event dropout rates: School years 2010-11 and 2011-12.* (NCES # 2014391). U.S. Department of Education. Washington, DC: National Center for Education Statistics. Retrieved from http://nces.ed.gov/pubsearch/pubsinfo.asp?pubid=2014391

Appendix A

Changes in Four-Year High School Graduation, Four-Year College Enrollment, and College Match Rates by Achievement

Changes in High School Graduation Rates by EXPLORE Score

From 2006 to 2014, high school graduation rates improved for students at all levels of incoming EXPLORE scores (**see Figure A.1**). The EXPLORE exam was administered in the fall of ninth grade. The graduation rate for students with the lowest EXPLORE scores—scoring below 12—increased by 17 percentage points in this time. A forthcoming UChicago CCSR research report examines the increases in high school graduation rates.

FIGURE A.1

CCSR Four-Year High School Graduation Rates Among First-Time Ninth-Graders, by Ninth-Grade EXPLORE Score

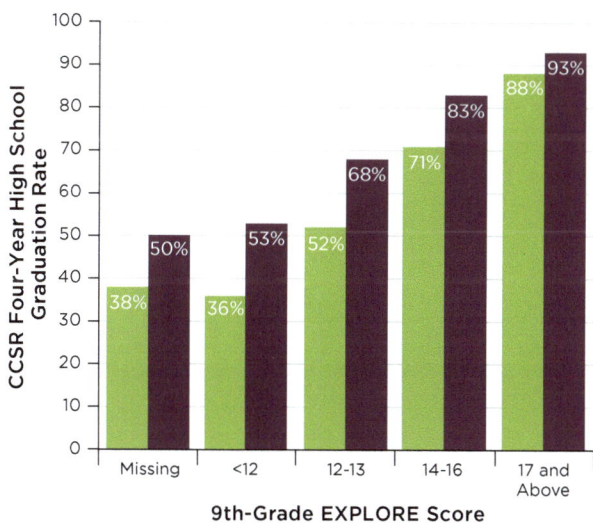

Legend:
- 2002 First-Time 9th-Graders Who Graduated High School by 2006
- 2010 First-Time 9th-Graders Who Graduated High School by 2014

Changes in Four-Year College Enrollment Rates by ACT Score and High School GPA

From 2006 to 2013, four-year college enrollment rates increased slightly for students at all levels of achievement on the ACT (**see Figure A.2**). Four-year college enrollment rates also increased for students in all GPA categories, except students who graduated with less than a 2.5 GPA (**see Figure A.3**).

FIGURE A.2

Enrollment Rates at Four-Year Colleges Among High School Graduates, by ACT Score

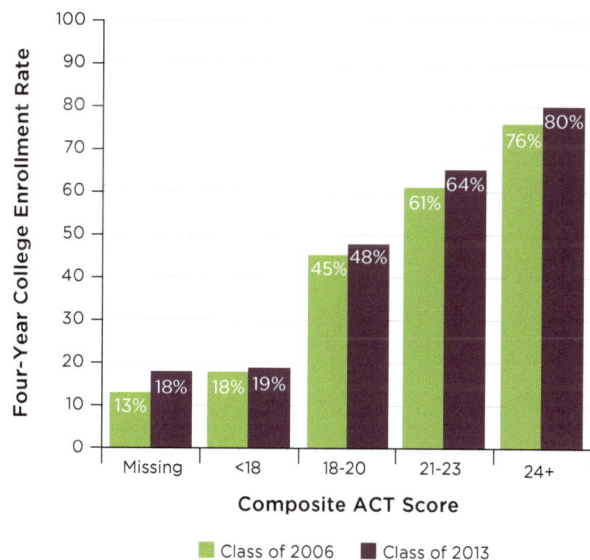

Legend:
- Class of 2006
- Class of 2013

FIGURE A.3

Enrollment Rates at Four-Year Colleges Among High School Graduates, by High School GPA

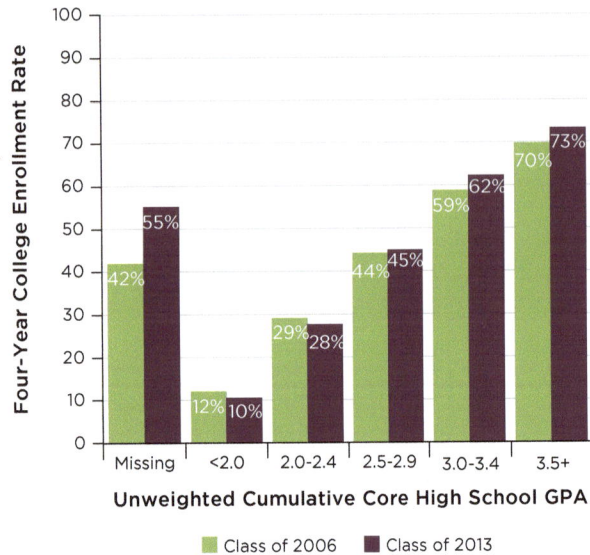

Unweighted Cumulative Core High School GPA

■ Class of 2006　■ Class of 2013

Note: The Missing category includes charter school graduates and students for whom we are missing course grades.

Changes in College Match Rates

A student's high school GPA and ACT score can be combined into an access category that identifies the selectivity level of colleges to which the student is likely to be admitted.[27] The rate at which students enroll in a college whose selectivity matches or exceeds their access category is referred to as the college match rate. **Figure A.4** shows how college match rates have changed among students with access to four-year colleges. See Roderick et al. (2008) for the combinations of ACT score and GPA that give students access to four-year colleges.

College match rates have declined slightly for all but the most highly qualified CPS graduates—those with access to very selective colleges. However, these trends should be interpreted with caution because we are unable to calculate college match rates for 21 percent of 2013 four-year college enrollees, compared to 3 percent in 2006. The increase in the percent of students missing the data necessary to calculate college match rates is due to the increase in the proportion of CPS students attending charter schools. Charter schools do not provide their students' course grades to CPS or UChicago CCSR.

FIGURE A.4

Percent of Graduates Who Enroll in a Match or Overmatch College, by Access Category

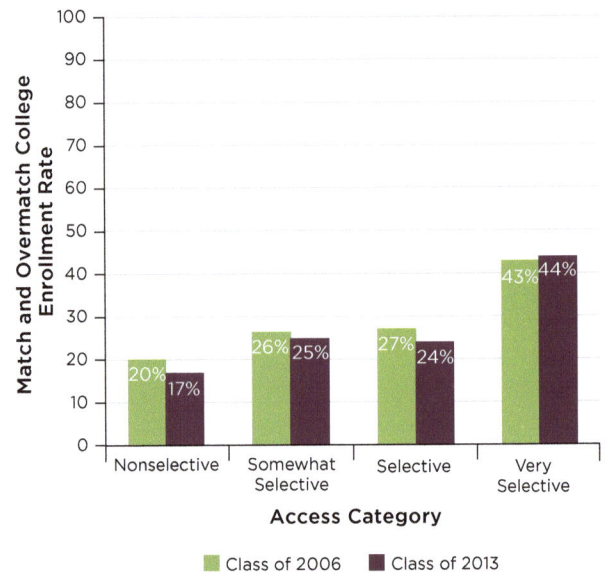

Access Category

■ Class of 2006　■ Class of 2013

Note: This figure does not include students who are in the two-year college access category or students for whom we are missing course grades.

---

26 Roderick et al. (2006); Roderick et al. (2008).

Appendix B
Data and Methods

Data Sources

UChicago CCSR's archive of CPS administrative records includes student demographics, test scores, course grades, and high school graduation records. With the exception of course grades used to compute GPAs, all of these data are available for charter school students.

Data from the National Student Clearinghouse (NSC) are used for all college enrollment and college graduation rates. The NSC houses enrollment and graduation records for colleges throughout the United States and covers 98 percent of all postsecondary enrollments nationally. Data on the institutional graduation rates of the colleges attended by CPS graduates are from the Integrated Postsecondary Education Data System (IPEDS), which collects data from all colleges that participate in federal student financial aid programs. Selectivity categories are based on ratings from *Barron's Profiles of American Colleges* (2012). All of these data are available for charter school graduates.

How We Calculated the Rates Reported in This Brief

All high school graduation rates reported in this brief refer to the proportion of first-time ninth-graders who earned a regular diploma in four years, including the summer after their fourth year. Students are considered a first-time ninth-grader if they had never before been enrolled in a CPS high school or Academic Preparatory Center (APC) and if they either a) were actively enrolled as a ninth-grader or APC student on the thirtieth day of the school year or b) enrolled as a ninth-grader after the thirtieth day of the school year and remained in a school long enough to receive grades. Charter schools are not required to provide data on their students' course grades to CPS, and so UChicago CCSR does not receive charter school students' grades. Students who enrolled in a charter school after the thirtieth day are included in the first-time ninth-grader cohort, even though we do not know if they remained enrolled long enough to receive grades. Students who transferred into CPS after ninth grade are included in the cohort that corresponds to their grade. Ungraded special education students, students whose first CPS enrollment is at an alternative school, and students who permanently transferred out of CPS are not included in first-time ninth-grader cohorts. Diplomas granted from alternative schools are not counted as regular diplomas.

All college enrollment rates reported in this document refer to the proportion of a CPS graduating class who enrolled in the fall after their high school graduation at a primarily baccalaureate degree-granting postsecondary institution that participates in the NSC. Graduating classes are defined by CPS when submitting student records to be matched to college records by NSC. We remove students who graduated from an alternative or special education school from the graduating class.

College graduation rates are calculated among students who enrolled in the fall after their high school graduation at a baccalaureate-granting institution that participates in the NSC. Students who enroll in the fourth, fifth, or sixth years after high school graduation in an institution that did not participate in NSC's Degree Verify program by four years after the high school graduation year are not included in these rates, as we are unable to determine conclusively whether these students earned a degree.

Appendix C

Bachelor's Degree Completion by ACT and High School GPA

Figure C.1 shows how bachelor's degree completion rates among CPS four-year college enrollees vary according to students' cumulative unweighted core high school GPA and ACT composite score. For example, students with an ACT of 21-23 have about a 50 percent chance of graduating college if their high school GPA is between 2.5 and 2.9. Yet, students with the same ACT scores of 21-23, but a high school GPA above a 3.0, graduate college at rates of nearly 70 percent or higher. More than 50 percent of four-year college enrollees with high school GPAs of 3.0 or better earn a degree, regardless of their ACT score.

Compared to ACT scores, high school GPA has a stronger predictive relationship with college graduation among four-year college enrollees. Using data from four-year college enrollees from the CPS graduating class of 2006, we fit a logistic regression model predicting bachelor's degree completion as a function of cumulative unweighted core high school GPA and ACT composite score, both standardized. This model produces a coefficient of 0.57 for ACT and a coefficient of 0.79 for GPA.

The above model does not account for the effects of colleges on degree completion. Because ACT scores and GPAs are also related to college admissions, and the college a student attends may influence their likelihood of graduating, we run the above model again and include college effects so that we can compare the outcomes of students within the same colleges. Controlling for college effects produces a coefficient of 0.46 for ACT and a coefficient of 0.80 for GPA. The decrease of the ACT coefficient suggests that the relationship between ACT scores and bachelor's degree completion operates, in part, through students' college access and choice. On the other hand, the relative stability of the GPA coefficient suggests that high school GPA remains a strong predictor of students' likelihood of completing a degree—even among students who attend the same college.

FIGURE C.1

Six-Year Bachelor's Degree Completion Rates Among 2006 CPS Four-Year College Enrollees, by High School GPA and ACT Score

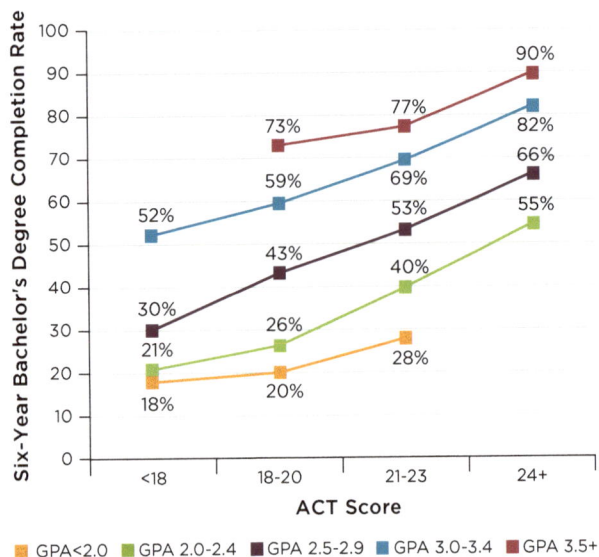

Note: Data points representing fewer than 100 students are not shown.

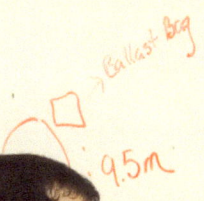

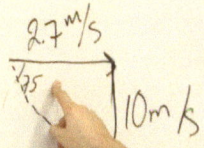

ABOUT THE AUTHORS

KALEEN HEALEY is a Senior Research Analyst at UChicago CCSR. She is currently developing data reports for CPS elementary and high schools for the To&Through Project. Her research interests include instructional improvement and the use of data in elementary schools. She holds a PhD in human development and social policy from Northwestern University.

JENNY NAGAOKA is the Deputy Director of UChicago CCSR, where she has conducted research for the past 15 years. Her research interests focus on urban education reform, particularly using data to connect research and practice and examining the school environments and instructional practices that promote college readiness and success. She has co-authored numerous journal articles and reports, including studies of college readiness, noncognitive factors, the transition from high school to postsecondary education, authentic intellectual instruction, and Chicago's initiative to end social promotion. Nagaoka received her BA from Macalester College and her master's of public policy degree from the Irving B. Harris School of Public Policy at the University of Chicago.

VALERIE MICHELMAN is a Research Analyst at UChicago CCSR. She earned a BA in economics and sociology from the University of Chicago. Current research interests include estimating the impact of health interventions on education outcomes, the implications of preschool and high school enrollment policies, and teachers' contributions to students' noncognitive skills.

UCHICAGOCCSR

www.ingramcontent.com/pod-product-compliance
Lightning Source LLC
Chambersburg PA
CBHW042112040426
42448CB00002B/234